Immune System Boosting

SMOOTHIES

Give Your Body What It Needs to Stay
Healthy – Quickly, Easily & Inexpensively

(Immune System Boosters
Book 2)

By Elena Garcia

Copyright ©Elena Garcia 2020

www.YourWellnessBooks.com

All cooking is an experiment in a sense, and many people come to the same or similar recipe over time. All recipes in this book have been derived from author's personal experience. Should any bear a close resemblance to those used elsewhere, that is purely coincidental.

The book is not intended to provide medical advice or to take the place of medical advice and treatment from your personal physician. Readers are advised to consult their own doctors or other qualified health professionals regarding the treatment of medical conditions. The author shall not be held liable or responsible for any misunderstanding or misuse of the information contained in this book. The information is not intended to diagnose, treat or cure any disease.

It is important to remember that the author of this book is not a doctor/ medical professional. Only opinions based upon her own personal experiences or research are cited. THE AUTHOR DOES NOT OFFER MEDICAL ADVICE or prescribe any treatments. For any health or medical issues – you should be talking to your doctor first.

Contents

Give Your Body What It Needs to Stay Healthy – Quickly, Easily & Inexpensively 8

Your Health Mindset – Focus on What You CAN Do 10

The 3 Pillars of Vibrant Health 18

Why Your Immune System Is Important And What It Does 24

Immune System Boosting Smoothies – All You Need to Know 25

The Most Vital Nutrients Your Immune System Boosting Smoothies Need 28

You Need Alkaline Minerals 34

Foods and Ingredients to Avoid in Your Smoothies 37

Creamy Low Carb High Fat Smoothie 41

Vitamin C Power Smoothie 42

Beautiful Skin Immunity Boost Smoothie 43

Optimal Cell Reparation Smoothie 44

Detox Your Body Healing Smoothie 46

Clean Liver Happy Immune System Smoothie 48

Antioxidant Power Smoothie 49

Low Carb Immune Energizer Smoothie 51

Sweet Dream Smoothie 53

Vitamin C Green Smoothie 54

Mediterranean Smoothie Meal 55

Chia Seed Pudding Smoothie 57

Spicy Meal Replacement Health Booster 59

Quinoa Immune System Booster 61

Simple Green Smoothie 63

Sweet Green Smoothie Energizer.............................64

Anti-Inflammation Warrior Smoothie 65

Mediterranean Breeze Smoothie 66

Cilantro Immune Boost Smoothie 67

Weigh Loss Immune System Mix Smoothie 68

Vegan Keto Energy Smoothie..................................69

Vitamin A Health Smoothie 71

Vitamin C PowerHouse Smoothie 72

Easy Relaxation Smoothie 73

Spicy Mediterranean Smoothie...............................74

Mood Boosting Smoothie 75

Protein Hormone Balancer 77

Simple Detox Spicy Smoothie 79

Ultimate Health Smoothie 81

Simple Cleanse Smoothie 83

Super Antioxidant Green Smoothie.........................84

Fill Me Up Smoothie..85

Sweet Veggie Smoothie..86

Green Energy Bowl..87

Anti-Flu Green Abundance Smoothie 89

Conclusion...91

Give Your Body What It Needs to Stay Healthy – Quickly, Easily & Inexpensively

Dear Reader, have you ever been told that all smoothies are super healthy and good for you?

If yes – keep reading because you have been lied to. You see, not all smoothies are made equal. And not all smoothies are healthy and good for you. Finally - not all smoothies are good for your immune system.

In fact, many so-called "healthy smoothies" may be weakening your immune system without you even realizing.

This is why we have created this little book. We want you to feel empowered and confident. We want you to know exactly what kind of smoothies to make to help you stay healthy while taking care of your body in an all-natural way.

It's time to revolutionize your wellbeing with immune system boosting smoothies!

Here's exactly what you will discover inside:

-Absolutely forbidden ingredients to NEVER use in your smoothies (unless you don't care about your health and immune system).

-Supposedly healthy smoothies you must stay away from, at all costs!

-The unusual nutrient combination that all immune system boosting smoothies need

-The WORST food whatsoever (and the number 1 immune system killer)

-The Mineral Quartet and what most smoothies overlook (+ a few simple tips to easily include the Mineral Quartet in your smoothies)

-Quick, easy and delicious smoothie recipes to help you take care of your immune system almost on autopilot

-Why taking another supplement (or a bunch of vitamins) will never cut it, unless you do this one thing...

You have the power to take care of your health and your immune system. I am very excited for you and your journey! We are in this together. Let's start off with mindset and motivation...

Your Health Mindset – Focus on What You CAN Do

We all want to stay healthy, vibrant, and energized. And we all want to feel confident knowing we are doing the right things to give our body what it needs to thrive.

The problem? Life can get busy and stressful. And when it does, we tend to put our health and self-care at the end of our "to-do-lists." Sometimes, we don't pay any attention to our health until we get a wake-up call (usually manifesting as a disease).

The good news? Taking care of your body through healthy habits and balanced lifestyle choices doesn't have to be hard. There are many effective diet tweaks that are simple to implement and have the power to strengthen your immune system.

So that you get sick less, and even when you do, you recover faster! As your body gets stronger and you start noticing the effects of your healthy choices, you develop more confidence in your body and its ability to heal.

The main reason why I decided to write this book is to empower you. Yes, I know you are busy! And I know that being 100% perfect with your diet, or following the latest "health fad" is not only impossible but also impractical.

Luckily, with the help of this little book, you can start taking meaningful action step-by-step.

So that you feel energized and get sick less. And so that you feel confident knowing you can take care of your body while doing everything you possibly can to keep it healthy.

Please note- the keyword here is "everything you POSSIBLY CAN." We are not talking about some magical cure books. Also, this book is not aimed at diagnosing or treating any health issues. It's not a medical book, and I am not your physician. As a wellness writer, I know my place, and ethical framework is critical to me. I don't like the hype, overnight miracles, or marketing claims.

This book focuses on empowerment, healthy lifestyle choices, and disease prevention through giving your body natural foods that are rich in substances that have been scientifically proven to strengthen your immune system.

And this my friend is true empowerment. You are focusing on what you can do instead of living in fear, neglect, or negativity.

Being positive is not only about positive thinking. It's more about taking positive action- whenever you can, to the best of your ability!

This book is your wellness self-help guide. You can start helping your body right here and right now. And you can do the best you can to make it stronger!

At the same time, please remember to visit your doctor regularly for checkups and blood work, etc. (even if you are healthy). That way, any imbalances or deficiencies can get detected earlier rather than later, and the path to recovery and healing can be much shorter. If you suffer from any existing health issues or are on medication, I highly recommend you consult your diet and lifestyle choices with your doctor.

"Oh, but come on, if it's natural, it's always good for me and safe, right?". Yes, most of the time, it is, especially if you are healthy and don't have any allergies and are not on medication.

But, you always want to make sure you stay on the safe side. Some natural herbs may interfere with certain medications, and some superfoods (even if they work great for 99.9999% of people who use them) may just not be the right choice for you and your body.

The best thing you can do for yourself is to combine the natural world and self-education (like, for example, this book or other wellness self-help guides like this one) with science and expertise from your health care provider or medical professional.

12

With that being said (or written, lol!), let's have a look at what is covered in this little booklet!

The Immune System Boosting Smoothies book is a simple blueprint you can follow even on a busy schedule, because smoothies are very quick to make. The best part? Many of the smoothie recipes in this book can be even used as a meal replacement. How cool is that?

This is the second book in the Immune System Boosters Series. The first book is *the Immune System Diet & Lifestyle.* After releasing it to our little Your Wellness Books community, I have quickly realized that out of the all immune system methods and recipes covered, most of our beloved Readers, loved smoothies!

And, I am not surprised at all. I myself am a big smoothie lover! As such, I have been passionately studying different smoothie-making methods for years. Finally, I came to a simple conclusion – not all smoothies are created equal! Yes, some smoothies may be great for some quick weight loss or detox. But...when it comes to taking care of your immune system- we need to step into a whole new game!

This is exactly what this book will help you with. It's as simple as learning what to put into your smoothies and what to avoid. Then, you also need to know what kind of vitamins and minerals are the best for your immune system, and which foods (that are blend-able, or, as my friend likes to call it – smoothie-make-able).

Oh, and you need to back it all up with powerful and meaningful action. From a place of faith, abundance and confidence.

Sometimes, people write to me and ask "Will IT work for me?". By "IT" they refer to some diet, recipes, or a nutritional system.

My response is usually – *Why are you asking*?
And, I will be honest here. I am very good at reading people's energies, even by the way they write. I can immediately know if a person asks "Will this work for me", from a place of curiosity, or from a place of "I have been doing some research, I came across this thing, and I am just curious, I felt like asking, why not?".

Or, if a person is asking the same question from a place of a victim mentality, everything happens to me, I can't do anything, nothing is worth it, I can't stick to anything, I am not worthy...

I also immediately know if a person is asking this question to give someone else the responsibility for their action (or the lack of it), or if a person simply wants to learn more. The methods, therapies, supplements, diets and nutritional systems are what they are. Just some methods. They will never work for you if you don't give them a try.

Also, true health transformations do take time! The key to success is simple. Focus on the process and enjoy the journey. We all have good days and bad days. Bad days make us less motivated to take healthy actions in alignment with our health goals. Absolutely normal!

But, not necessarily, acceptable. So, I invite you to step into your higher self, your healthier self and start taking healthy action today.

How about one delicious immune system boosting smoothie a day?

Then, slowly back up your daily smoothies with a clean food diet you love. Add some daily walks, or relaxation. Listen to your body, tune in for the answers.

Let's do this!

Before we dive into the smoothies, I would love to invite you to join our VIP Wellness Newsletter.

When you do, you will receive this free complimentary guide (not available on Amazon or other online stores):

www.yourwellnessbooks.com/newsletter

You will also be the first one to be notified about your new books & audiobooks (at deeply discounted prices) + receive our best health and weight loss tips to help you achieve your goals!

Join now and become a successful reader at no cost:
www.yourwellnessbooks.com/newsletter

The 3 Pillars of Vibrant Health

It all starts with empowerment. That inner feeling that maybe there is something you can do to help yourself. That perhaps, there is something more out there. That maybe, you can transform your body and mind and become a healthier version of yourself.

And congrats to You, My Friend! If you are reading this book, chances are you are already empowered! For some reason, you decided to let go of skepticism, and you picked up this little booklet because you believe in yourself, and you know you can help yourself.

Most people never take this step. They believe that things just happen. They think there is good luck and bad luck, or that it's all about genetics. And, yes, there is some truth to that. As I already said, we can't control everything. But true empowerment is all about focusing on what we can do, right here and right now.

I don't know about You, but I leave the rest to the Higher Power and prayer (I don't want to get too philosophical here, so I will just skip this part for now). The bottom line is – always focus on what you can control and see adverse circumstances as a challenge to make you stronger and motivate you to do something different.

This is what I like to call the True Empowerment!
And this is our First Pillar of Health. When you feel
empowered, you focus on what you can control. And
what you focus on expands.

You see, your mind works like a search engine. Imagine
you go on Google and YouTube and type in a diet, let's say
it's the keto diet or some other diet. You can type in "keto
success stories," to see how it worked for other people
and how much weight they have lost. Or you can type in
"keto scam," or something else. Both are fine. There is no
right or wrong.

The only thing I want you to pay attention to is your mind
and how it works. If you focus on why something will not
work for you and is not worth doing -your mind (just like a
Google search engine), will find the evidence to back it up.
And at the same time, if you focus on why something
does work, you will also find the evidence to back it up as
well.

What you decide to focus on is up to you! Personally, I
always intend to focus on the positive, while not staying
ignorant of the negative. For example, while studying a
new herb, I want to be open to all its amazing health
benefits, but I also want to know the possible side effects
to stay on the safe side.

However, I don't choose to focus on the negative 100%, because that would make me depressed, and I would never do or try anything new to improve my health.

Unfortunately, some people are like that. Nothing can spark their interest. Exercise is not worth it; healthy herbal teas are not worth it; eating more vegetables and fruits - not worth it.

Yes, we will all die. But, as long as we are here, why not enjoy energy and vitality and be grateful for the fact that we are here? Why not show the God, the Universe/ the Higher Power (whatever your belief is) that because we are grateful we are here- we do the best we can, whenever we can so that we can take care of ourselves?

Stay empowered and inspired by focusing on what you can control, right here, right now!

The second pillar of health is..
Taking Inspired Action backed up by patience and belief.
No action, no results. It's as simple as that! Now, I will be the first one to admit that I have been guilty of paralysis by analysis. I like reading and researching. And so, I spent many years just reading about weight loss and different diets, but would never take action on the information I studied! Until one day, I had a wake-up call. I was on a weight loss forum, and I got involved in a discussion about a diet X and why it works and why diet Y was better. I was there, kind of trolling around and sharing my opinions in a negative way.

Until this young fit girl, who was a weight loss coach, asked me- *Ok, if you know so much about it, please tell us how much weight you lost and how many people you helped to lose weight. Otherwise, stop talking about the things you haven't done yourself. You are just judging and criticizing others!*

At first, I felt so pissed off. How come, this young girl, who probably doesn't have all this knowledge that I have is telling me what to do?

Well, she was right, and she put me in my place. I was just talking about the things I have read about in books, but I have never tried any of them.

Now, I am a different person, and I don't get involved in internet discussions about nutrition. And, even if I did, I would only share my own experience based on what I did and what worked or didn't work (and I would be kind to others).

So, from my own experience, and mindset transformation, I can honestly tell you that taking action (even imperfect) is all you need to focus on. When you read about this great superfood, ask yourself: *Ok, so how can I add it to my diet, quickly and painlessly?*

It doesn't have to be all or nothing. But, unfortunately, in our health community, many people go for all or nothing. I am super healthy and eat 100% clean (or follow this new diet 100%), or I eat fast food and tell myself that staying healthy is too hard!

The choice is always yours; you can always choose. But my number one tip for you is – take imperfect massive action and just do something today. Show your mind that you work with it, not against it. Nobody is perfect; it's not about being perfect; it's about PROGRESS!

So, to sum up, our first pillar is Empowerment. Then, we have to take Meaningful Action (the best we can, while letting go of perfection).

Finally, the Third Pillar is KISS!
Keep It Super Simple!

We are talking simple recipes and habits that will make your healthy lifestyle super enjoyable and fun! The KISS smoothies contained in this book are specifically designed to help you strengthen your immune system and enjoy a healthy, stress-free, and energized life.

Your Immune System Needs Your Help

When it comes to protecting yourself from diseases and viruses, you already know the following:

Wash your hands, use sanitizer, avoid shaking hands and hugging...etc

Great advice for sure...But- you already know this!
The problem is that nobody is talking about the most important thing you can do, which is to strengthen and fortify your immune system.

Why?

Why Your Immune System Is Important And What It Does

The role of the immune system is to protect your body from any foreign matters or substances that might cause any damage or imbalance while damaging the homeostasis. The effectiveness of your immune system depends on its ability to discriminate between foreign (nonself) and host(self) cells. When an organism is threatened by viruses or other harmful microorganisms, the immune system acts to provide protection. Usually, the immune system does not initiate a response against self.

At the same time, the lack of an immune response is called tolerance.

When a foreign matter or a virus enters your body, your defense system recognizes this as foreign through the immune system. Each cell in your body carries a mixture of proteins and sugars that serve to identify the cell to the immune system. Foreign objects lack the identifiers that all of the body's cells have, but each one has unique features or antigens where the immune system attaches identifiers called antibodies.

This is the basis for the specific defense mechanisms. Once you have built the antibodies for a specific antigen, the immune system will respond faster than if there had been no previous exposure to the antigen (i.e. you are immune to the pathogen, but only that specific pathogen, because your immune system responds faster.)

The non-specific part of the immune system is mostly composed of phagocytes (eating-cells), which engulf and digest foreign substances like bacteria and viruses, which do not bear the body's specific identifiers.

|

Immune System Boosting Smoothies – All You Need to Know

So, let's get started and get your body strong, healthy, and protected as much as possible!

Your beautiful immune system is so powerful and effective (when given the right fuel and taken care of).

It is so smart! It is vital to so many functions in your body, and most importantly – what you eat, drink, and your lifestyle directly impacts how well it functions and how well it protects you from foreign invaders that can result in disease.

Here's the sad truth…When you are stressed, and you have been eating a processed fast-food diet while getting poor sleep, you're more likely to pick up a bug, cough, cold or the flu.

And when you get sick and your body is unhealthy, it takes much longer to heal and recover.

Also, when it comes to viruses…If they attack your body, your immune system will try to defend it.

If your immune system is compromised, then you stand more chance of succumbing to illness. If it's healthy, it will have a better chance of fighting it off. Simple, right?

The Most Vital Nutrients Your Immune System Boosting Smoothies Need

Here's what your body needs to stay strong:
-Vitamin C,
-Zinc,
-Curcumin,
-Vitamin D
-Greens and Chlorophyll
-Alkaline Minerals such as Magnesium (they also help prevent anxiety and boost focus and relaxation to that you can sleep better)
-Simple Power Superfoods such as: Garlic, Ginger and Turmeric

And yes, you could just take some supplements and be done with the rest of this book.

But, here's one thing to understand: quality supplements from reputable brands can be costly. At the same time, even the most expensive and quality supplements can't guarantee proper absorption. If your body is out of balance, chances are, some vitamins and supplements may not absorb properly. Or, you may overdo them and imbalance something else.

Don't get me wrong- I have nothing against supplements and vitamins. But, I would turn to them only if recommended and prescribed by my doctor (as the last remedy).

The good news is that you can feed your body with an abundance of Vitamin C, as well as zinc, curcumin, and Vitamin D, by optimizing your nutrition. If that step doesn't help, and if your blood work will prove you are deficient in any of the vitamins mentioned above and nutrients, then talk to your doctor about supplementation.

If you are already taking any supplements and having success with it- keep it up.

All I want to open your eyes to is the power of natural and balanced nutrition. These are the immune system basics that can be implemented quite affordably (and naturally).

Multiple studies have proven all four of these to be effective in preventing, reducing the severity and reducing the length of colds & flu, because they directly support the immune system.

So now, let's have a closer look at some of them.

VITAMIN C
Since bodies do not produce or store the water-soluble vitamin C., we need to replenish our supply of vitamin C

every day. The best natural source is from fruits and vegetables, especially the following:

-orange,

-kiwi,

-lemon,

-guava,

- grapefruit,

-broccoli,

-cauliflower,

-red bell peppers

-papaya

-strawberries

-cantaloupe

I recommend going for fresh, seasonal fruits and veggies. Also, when it comes to fruit, my personal choice is to focus on low sugar fruits (such as lemons or grapefruits) more than other fruit that is rich in sugar (such as oranges or kiwis).

Of course, it's all about balance. But, I like to make sure I follow a low sugar diet for the most part (more on that later).

Zinc

Zinc metabolizes nutrients while maintaining your immune system and growing/ repairing your body tissues.

Your body doesn't store zinc, so you need to eat enough every day to ensure you're meeting your daily requirements.

There are many delicious zinc-rich foods you can add to your diet (both plant-based and animal-based), such as:

1. Meat and shellfish.
2. Legumes (great alternative for vegans and vegetarians).
3. Seeds and nuts.
4. Eggs.
5. Dark chocolate and cocoa (yummy!)

Of course, blending meat or eggs would be a bit weird. So, would be blending lentils!

But, you can easily add some nuts and seeds to your smoothies- not only will your smoothies be more nutritious. You will also be able to stay full for hours!

More ideas to add more zinc-rich foods to your smoothies:
-you can start adding some zinc-rich foods to your smoothies, whenever possible. For example:
-add a bit of dark chocolate or cocoa powder to your fruit vitamin-C rich smoothies (for example oranges, cocoa, coconut milk, and kiwi).

-add some hard-boiled eggs or meat/seafood leftovers to your vegetable vitamin-C rich smoothies (you can also use legumes, such as lentils or chickpeas, or nuts and seeds) (for example: a smoothie made of red bell peppers, avocado, Himalayan salt, and some fresh tomato juice, can be made more filling by adding in some zinc-rich foods such as meat or seafood leftovers).

It's all about being creative and proactive. One simple meal can nourish your body with both Vitamin C and zinc while helping you save hours spent in your kitchen (and hundreds of dollars on expensive supplements that will not be effective anyways unless you take care of your diet first).

Now, let's move on to the next of our Immune System boosting ingredient – **Curcumin**.

Curcumin is the key active ingredient in turmeric. It can be easily added to your diet through teas or smoothies.

I usually buy fresh turmeric root and add it to my herbal teas, soups or smoothies. Sometimes, I use a powdered curcumin supplement (with a little bit of black pepper) and also add it to my Vitamin C rich smoothies.

For example:
2 oranges + 1-inch grated turmeric (peeled)+ 1-inch ginger (peeled) + 1 tablespoon coconut oil + 1 cup coconut milk and a bit of cinnamon.

Blend and enjoy!

Pro tip – whenever peeling turmeric, be sure to use hand gloves to protect your fingers and nails from going orange!

<u>Garlic – The Most Powerful Natural Antibiotic</u>
Garlic is a powerful immune-booster, mostly because of the compound allicin. Garlic has been shown to lower LDL cholesterol; it's a powerful antibiotic and anti-viral.

However, the allicin is hugely present in RAW garlic, and it disappears quickly once it's exposed to air or cooked.

So, if you want to use garlic to boost your immune system, I highly recommend focusing on raw garlic. You can easily do it by adding it to your immune system boosting veggie smoothies!

Avocado -Another Effective Immune-System Boosting Superfood

I highly recommend you increase your intake of healthy fats (omega 3 and saturated fat from coconut oil or avocado) to support your overall health and immunity.

Avocado contains the highest concentration of L-glutathione, known as the "master antioxidant". Glutathione is essential because it enables all other antioxidants to function, protect cells against free radical damage, and detoxifies the body of pollutants and other toxins.

It's also very rich in Magnesium to help your body stay in balance.
-Add them to your smoothies! You can make delicious and naturally creamy, super healthy smoothies such as:
1 avocado + 1 cup of nut milk + a bit of cinnamon powder + a few banana slices (so yummy and healthy!).

You Need Alkaline Minerals

There is no way around it; you just need them. Every day. Especially if you want to stay vibrant and full of energy.

Alkaline minerals include:

-calcium

-potassium

-magnesium

-sodium

Most people get enough calcium, but not enough potassium and sodium. And, most people are magnesium deficient. Yes, some supplementation (if prescribed by your doctor) can help, but if your body is out of balance, it may be hard to absorb them.

A natural, clean food approach is the best long-term remedy!

The first thing you can start implementing is to use Himalayan salt. I use it for all my meals, and sometimes I like to add it to my water.

Lemon water, to be specific, lemons are also very rich in alkaline minerals. They are naturally low sugar fruits.

At the same time, you want to start adding more greens to your diet, for example:
-spinach
-kale
-arugula
-basil
-parsley
-cilantro

These can be sneaked into your smoothies.

Here is my low carb and low sugar smoothie template:

- *1 avocado, peeled and pitted*
- *1 cup coconut or nut milk*
- *1 teaspoon chia seeds*
- *A few lime slices (you can also use lemons or grapefruits)*
- *A handful of greens of your choice*
- *1 teaspoon coconut oil*
- *A pinch of Himalayan salt*

Blend well, serve, and enjoy!

Chlorophyll and Greens

These are simple and inexpensive! Chlorophyll has the power to detox our body and help it heal faster. Leafy greens are also very important in alkaline minerals (that you already know are very important).

Foods and Ingredients to Avoid in Your Smoothies

Food to Avoid #1: SUGAR

Sugar is the most pro-inflammatory, immune-suppressing, hormone-unbalancing substance ever created. In fact, it's more addictive than cocaine!

If you want to stay healthy and take care of your immune system, quit the sugar or reduce it as much as possible.

The problem? If you eat processed and packaged foods – the sugar is almost everywhere. Then, milk and dairy products also contain sugar. So do fruit juices (even home-made)!

Hence, my earlier tip – fruit is good for you as it's rich in Vitamin C your immune system needs every day.

However, try to focus on low-sugar fruit more than high-sugar-fruit.

Sugar is always *sugar. Your body doesn't care where it's coming from. It treats all forms and sources of sugar equally.*

Let's compare these 2 smoothies:
Smoothie #1 is made of: 2 bananas, half cup dates, 2 cups milk or yoghurt and 1 apple.

Smoothie #2 is made of: low sugar fruit, avocado, nuts, nut milk and healthy greens (plus some turmeric powder).

Which smoothie do you think is healthier?
Of course - smoothie #2.
You see, smoothie #1 is loaded with sugar, lactose and carbs. Not very good for you or for your immune system.

Healthy Immune System Smoothie Boosting Template
-vitamin C rich fruits and veggies
-focus on low sugar fruits (other fruit is fine in moderation, unless you are diabetic or suffer from similar health conditions).
-add in some healthy greens
-avoid lactose products, focus on nut milk instead (use quality brands, with no added sugar)
-add in good fats (for example- avocado or coconut oil)
-avoid "over-carbing" your smoothies with too much fruit and avoid smoothies made ONLY with fruit. Instead, combine fruit with some greens and other healthy, immune system-boosting ingredients.

Now, let's dive into the recipes!

Measurements Used in the Recipes

The cup measurement I use is the American Cup measurement.

I also use it for dry ingredients. If you are new to it, let me help you:

If you don't have American Cup measures, just use a metric or imperial liquid measuring jug and fill your jug with your ingredient to the corresponding level. Here's how to go about it:

1 American Cup= 250ml= 8 fl.oz.
For example:
If a recipe calls for 1 cup of almonds, simply place your almonds into your measuring jug until it reaches the 250 ml/8oz marks.

Quite easy, right?

I know that different countries use different measurements, and I wanted to make things simple for you. I have also noticed that very often, those who are used to American Cup measurements complain about metric measurements and vice versa. However, if you apply what I have just explained, you will find it easy to use both.

Creamy Low Carb High Fat Smoothie

This smoothie is naturally creamy and very tasty. Not only is it a fantastic, natural remedy to help you boost your immune system. It's also a great weight loss smoothie! The cinnamon powder makes this smoothie nice and sweet. Coconut oil will help you reduce sugar cravings.

Serves: 1-2
Ingredients:
Liquid:
- 1 tablespoon coconut oil
- 2 tablespoons fresh lime juice
- 2 cups cold coconut milk, unsweetened

Dry:
- A handful of cashews, raw, soaked in filtered water for at least a few hours
- 1 tablespoon chia seeds
- 1 small avocado, peeled and pitted

Other:
- Half teaspoon ginger powder
- Optional- stevia to sweeten
- 1 teaspoon cinnamon powder

Instructions:
1. Blend all the ingredients using a blender.
2. Process until smooth.
3. Serve and enjoy!

Vitamin C Power Smoothie

This original smoothie tastes a bit like Greek yogurt but is entirely plant-based and dairy-free.

Serves: 1-2
Ingredients:
Liquid:
- 2 cups cold unsweetened almond milk
- 1 tablespoon avocado oil

Dry:
- 1 small lemon, peeled and sliced
- 1 small avocado, peeled and pitted
- 2 tablespoons chia seeds (or chia seed powder)
- 1-inch ginger, peeled
- A few slices of red bell pepper

Other:
- a few lime slices to garnish
- a pinch of Himalayan salt
- a pinch of black pepper to taste

Instructions:
1. Place all the ingredients in a blender.
2. Blend until smooth. Serve and enjoy!

Beautiful Skin Immunity Boost Smoothie

This beautiful smoothie is designed to help you have a super healthy-looking, glowing skin while boosting your immunity at the same time!

Serves: 1-2
Ingredients:
Liquid:

- 1 cup coconut milk
- Half cup of coconut water (or normal filtered water)

Dry:

- 3 small carrots, peeled
- 1 big red bell pepper, cut into smaller pieces
- 2 tablespoons chia seeds

Other:

- 1 teaspoon cinnamon powder
- stevia to sweeten if needed
- fresh mint leaves and lime slices to serve

Instructions:

1. Place all the ingredients in a blender.
2. Blend until smooth.
3. Pour into a glass and enjoy!

Optimal Cell Reparation Smoothie

If you want to boost your immune system and heal your body, you gotta explore moringa, mint, and cilantro! Moringa is a natural protein green superfood. It contains all the essential amino acids – the building blocks of protein- that are needed to grow, repair, and maintain cells. At the same time, it's rich in alkaline minerals such as magnesium, iron, and potassium.

Serves: 1-2
Ingredients:
Liquid:
- 1 cup of coconut milk
- Half cup coconut water

Dry:
- Handful of almonds, soaked in filtered water for at least a few hours
- 1-inch fresh ginger, peeled
- A few avocado slices
- Half grapefruit, peeled

Other:
- 1 teaspoon moringa powder
- A handful of fresh mint
- A handful of fresh cilantro leaves

Instructions:

1. Place all the ingredients into a blender
2. Process well until smooth. Enjoy!

Detox Your Body Healing Smoothie

This smoothie is perfect as a quick detox smoothie so that you can get rid of toxins and boost your immunity. It's creamy, delicious and fun!

Servings: 2-3
Ingredients:
Liquid:
- 1 cup almond milk
- Half cup water, filtered
- 1 tablespoon coconut oil

Dry:
- 2 big cucumbers, peeled and roughly sliced
- 1 big avocado, peeled and pitted
- A handful of cilantro leaves
- 1 tablespoon almond or hemp seed protein powder
- Half lemon, peeled and sliced
- 4 tablespoons almonds, chopped or powdered

Other:
- Pinch of Himalayan salt to taste
- Pinch of black pepper to taste
- 2 tablespoons chive, chopped

- 1 teaspoon spirulina powder, or other green powder such as Organifi (you can learn more at: www.yourwellnessbooks.com/supplements)

Instructions:
1. Place all the ingredients in a blender.
2. Blend well and pour into a smoothie glass or a small soup bowl (feel free to add in some protein if you want).
3. Serve and enjoy!

Clean Liver Happy Immune System Smoothie

This recipe is just perfect as a quick breakfast smoothie to help you take care of your liver first thing in the morning. It's rich in Vitamin C, zinc and good fats to boost your immune system and feel amazing.

Servings: 1-2
Ingredients:
Liquid:

- 1 cup almond or other nut milk
- Half cup of water, filtered

Dry:

- Half cup radish
- 1 small avocado, peeled and pitted
- A handful of fresh arugula leaves
- 1 orange, peeled
- 1 red apple, peeled

Other:

- Pinch of Himalaya salt to taste
- 1 teaspoon spirulina (or other green powder)

Instructions:

1. Blend all the ingredients.
2. Serve and enjoy!

Antioxidant Power Smoothie

Cilantro is a very often overlooked green herb with potent antioxidant properties. Most people think it's only for curries and spicy dishes. But... it tastes great in smoothies too and is a true immune system miracle!

Servings: 2-3
Ingredients
Liquid:
- 2 cups coconut milk or almond milk
- 1 tablespoon coconut oil

Dry:
- A handful of fresh cilantro leaves
- 2 small carrots, peeled
- Half avocado, peeled and pitted
- 1 green banana, peeled
- A handful of baby spinach leaves

Other:
- half teaspoon ginger powder
- 1 teaspoon moringa powder
- Half teaspoon cinnamon powder
- Pinch of Himalaya salt to taste

Instructions:

1. Combine all the ingredients in a blender.
2. Process until smooth.
3. Pour into a smoothie glass or a small soup bowl and enjoy!

Low Carb Immune Energizer Smoothie

This smoothie is the perfect recipe to fill you up and help you stay energized for hours. It's rich in Vitamin C, zinc and good fats. It also sneaks in some ginger and turmeric!

Servings: 2
Ingredients:
Liquid:

- 1 cup of coconut milk
- Half cup cashew milk
- 2 teaspoons coconut oil

Dry:

- 1 big avocado, peeled, pitted and sliced
- Half lemon, peeled and sliced
- A handful of cashews
- A handful of almonds
- 1-inch turmeric, peeled
- 1-inch ginger, peeled

Other:

- 1 teaspoon spirulina or other green powder
- Stevia to taste if needed

Instructions:

1. Place all the ingredients in a blender.
2. Process until smooth.
3. Serve in a smoothie glass and garnish with a few lime slices.
4. Drink to your health, and enjoy!

Sweet Dream Smoothie

This smoothie is naturally sweet and very nutritious.
Perfect for a healthy dessert!

Serves: 1-2
Ingredients:
Liquid:

- 1 cup coconut milk or other nut/ plant-based milk
- 1 tablespoon coconut oil

Dry:

- 2 small oranges, peeled and cut into smaller pieces
- 1-inch ginger, peeled
- 1 tablespoon chia seeds

Other:

- 1 teaspoon cinnamon powder
- Optional: stevia to sweeten

Instructions:

1. Place all the ingredients in a blender.
2. Process well until smooth.
3. If needed, sweeten with stevia.

Vitamin C Green Smoothie

This smoothie combines spinach and oranges to help you boost your energy naturally (vitamin C and iron is an excellent combo!).

Serves: 1-2
Ingredients:
Liquid:
- 2 cups coconut milk or any other plant-based or nut milk

Dry:
- Half avocado, peeled, pitted and sliced
- Half cup mixed greens (I like spinach or arugula, or both)
- 2 oranges, peeled
- 2 tablespoons chia seeds or other seeds of your choice

Instructions:
1. Place all the ingredients in a blender.
2. Process well until smooth.
3. Enjoy!

Mediterranean Smoothie Meal

This recipe is similar to the original Spanish gazpacho recipe – super healthy and a great addition to your immune system boosting remedies. The best part? You can also use this smoothie as a meal replacement (and add in some quality protein – plant or animal based).

Serves: 2
Ingredients:
Liquid:

- 1 cup water, filtered
- 1 cup cashew or almond milk
- 2 tablespoons extra virgin, organic olive oil (or avocado oil)

Dry:

- 8 small radishes
- 1 big green bell pepper, roughly chopped
- A few onion rings
- 2 garlic cloves, peeled
- 3 big tomatoes, roughly chopped
- 3 big cucumbers, peeled
- 2 slices of lime, peel removed

Other:
- 2 generous pinches of Himalayan salt
- Half teaspoon oregano
- Half teaspoon black pepper
- Half teaspoon basil (or a few fresh basil leaves)
- Half teaspoon parsley (or a few fresh parsley leaves)

To serve:
- 1-2 tablespoons fresh lemon juice to serve
- 1-2 tablespoons chopped chive to serve

Instructions:
1. Place all the ingredients in a blender.
2. Process well until smooth.
3. Taste to see if you need to add any more herbs, spices, or Himalayan salt.
4. Serve in a small soup bowl, adding in some fresh lemon juice and fresh chive.
5. Feel free to add some protein (hard boiled eggs, meat or fish leftovers, or lentils/chickpeas are great for that!).
6. Enjoy!

Chia Seed Pudding Smoothie

This simple immune system boosting smoothie is based mostly on herbs and spices. Chia seeds bring in some important nutrients. They are an excellent source of omega-3 fatty acids, rich in antioxidants. They also offer an abundance of fiber, iron, and calcium. Just perfect for an all-natural immune system boosting smoothie.

Serves: 1-2
Ingredients:
- 1 cup coconut milk, unsweetened
- Juice of 1 lime

Dry:
- 1 tablespoon chia seeds
- A handful of cashews
- 1 big banana, peeled
- A few dates, pitted

Other:
- Half teaspoon cinnamon powder
- 1 generous pinch of nutmeg powder
- A few fresh mint leaves

Instructions:
1. Place all the ingredients in a blender.
2. Process until smooth.

3. Now, try the smoothie to see if you like the taste.
4. If needed, add in some stevia and blend again.
5. Place in a smoothie glass, drink, and enjoy!

Spicy Meal Replacement Health Booster

This smoothie is just perfect for a quick lunch or dinner!

Serves: 2
Ingredients:
Liquid:

- 1 cup of coconut milk or almond milk
- 1 cup water, filtered

Dry:

- 1 big garlic clove, peeled
- 1-inch turmeric, peeled
- 2 tablespoons raw almonds, soaked in water for at least a few hours
- 2 sweet potatoes, peeled and cooked
- 1 big tomato, cut into smaller pieces
- A few onion rings

Other:

- A pinch of cumin powder
- A pinch of black pepper powder
- 1 tablespoon extra-virgin, organic olive oil or avocado oil (cold-pressed)
- 1 tablespoon lime juice, to serve
- A big handful of fresh cilantro leaves
- A big handful of fresh parsley leaves
- A generous pinch of Himalayan salt

- A pinch red chili powder

Instructions:
1. Place all the ingredients in a blender.
2. Process until smooth.
3. Serve in a big smoothie glass or a soup bowl.
4. Sprinkle over some lime juice and enjoy!

Quinoa Immune System Booster

Quinoa alone is a natural immune system-boosting ingredient! It's naturally gluten-free and high in protein. Even though it's a plant-based food, it contains sufficient amounts of all nine essential amino acids. In addition to that, it's also high in fiber, magnesium, B vitamins, iron, potassium, calcium, phosphorus, vitamin E (as well as numerous antioxidants).

Serves: 1-2
Ingredients:
Liquid:

- 1 cup coconut milk, unsweetened
- 1 cup almond milk, unsweetened

Dry:

- Half cup of quinoa, cooked
- 2 big cucumbers, peeled and cut into smaller pieces
- A few slices of avocado
- 1 small garlic clove, peeled

Other:

- A pinch of cumin powder
- A pinch of curry powder
- A big handful of cilantro leaves
- A pinch of Himalayan salt

Instructions:

1. Blend all the ingredients in a blender.
2. Serve and enjoy!

Simple Green Smoothie

Arugula is rich in calcium and iron as well as vitamin A, and it tastes great in smoothies!

Serves: 1-2
Ingredients:
Liquid:
- 1 cup of coconut milk
- 1 cup rooibos tea infusion, cooled down

Dry:
- A handful of cilantro leaves
- 1 tablespoon chia seeds or chia seed powder
- 1 cup fresh arugula leaves
- A handful of fresh parsley leaves

Other:
- A pinch of black pepper powder
- A pinch of oregano
- A pinch of Himalayan salt
- A pinch of chili powder

Instructions:
1. Place all the ingredients in a blender.
2. Blend well until smooth.
3. Serve in a smoothie glass and enjoy!

Sweet Green Smoothie Energizer

If you are having a hard time drinking green smoothies, this recipe will help you get started. It's very comforting because of its naturally sweet taste and creaminess.

Servings: 2
Ingredients:
Liquid:
- 1 cup hazelnut milk

Dry:
- 1 cup spinach leaves
- 1 small green banana
- A few dates, pitted
- A handful of hazelnuts

Other:
- 1 tablespoon cinnamon powder
- Stevia to sweeten if needed
- Optional: cocoa powder

Instructions:
1. Place all the ingredients through a blender.
2. Process well until smooth and creamy. If needed, add some water.
3. Serve and enjoy!

Anti-Inflammation Warrior Smoothie

This recipe combines fresh cherries which are known for their high antioxidant properties with naturally sweet and vitamin C rich red bell peppers. Ginger adds to anti-inflammatory properties and immune system-boosting properties.

Servings: 2
Ingredients:
Liquid:
- 1 cup coconut water

Dry:
- Half cup of fresh cherries, pitted
- 1 big red bell pepper, chopped, seeds removed
- 2-inch ginger, peeled

Other:
- Half teaspoon maca powder
- 1 teaspoon chia seeds

Instructions:
1. Place all the ingredients through a blender.
2. Process well until smooth and creamy. If needed, add some water.
3. Serve and enjoy!

Mediterranean Breeze Smoothie

Tomatoes are high in vitamin C, antioxidants and essential minerals. Avocados add in potassium and essential fats.

Servings: 2
Ingredients:
Liquid:
- 2 cups water, filtered
- 1 tablespoon extra-virgin olive oil

Dry:
- 1 cup cherry tomatoes
- 1 green bell pepper, chopped, seeds removed
- 1 ripe avocado, halved and pitted
- 1 garlic clove, peeled
- Half cup green olives, pitted

Other:
- 1 teaspoon fresh rosemary and thyme
- 1 tablespoon raw pistachio nuts
- Himalaya salt and black pepper to taste

Instructions:
1. Place all the ingredients through a blender.
2. Process well until smooth and creamy. If needed, add more water.
3. Serve and enjoy!

Cilantro Immune Boost Smoothie

Cilantro is a great source of essential minerals and dietary fiber. The chia seeds add a healthy dose of fats and the cashew nuts provide the protein, as well as a little extra healthy fat.

Servings: 2
Ingredients:
Liquid:

- 1 cup of coconut milk

Dry:

- Half cup fresh cilantro leaves, well rinsed and dried off with kitchen towel
- 1 cucumber, peeled and sliced
- A handful of raw cashew nuts

Other:

- 1 tablespoon chia seeds
- Himalaya salt and black pepper to taste
- Half teaspoon turmeric powder

Instructions:

1. Place all the ingredients through a blender.
2. Process well until smooth and creamy. If needed, add some water.
3. Serve and enjoy!

Weigh Loss Immune System Mix Smoothie

Himalaya salt makes this green smoothie taste delicious. You can also spice it up with some chili, curry, black pepper or cilantro!

What I really like about this smoothie is that it's great as a natural immune system booster, and it's also fantastic for weight loss.

Servings: 3-4
Ingredients:

- 2 cups coconut milk (unsweetened)
- 2 small avocados, peeled and pitted
- 1 big cucumber, peeled and chopped
- A handful of spinach
- Pinch of Himalaya salt to taste

Instructions:

1. Place all the ingredients in a blender.
2. Blend well.
3. Serve as a smoothie or a raw soup and enjoy!

Vegan Keto Energy Smoothie

This smoothie combines the best of keto, vegan and paleo worlds! It tastes very refreshing and can also be served as a raw, healing soup.

Servings: 1-2
Ingredients:
Liquid:
- 1 cup thick coconut milk
- 1 tablespoon coconut oil

Dry:
- 1 avocado, peeled and pitted
- 1 small lime, peeled
- 2 tablespoons chia seeds or chia seed powder

Other:
- Half teaspoon curry powder
- Himalaya salt to taste (optional)

Instructions:
1. Blend all the ingredients.
2. Pour your smoothie into a smoothie glass or a small soup bowl.
3. Sprinkle more curry powder or other spices on top.
4. Enjoy!

Vitamin A Health Smoothie

This creamy smoothie is a fantastic source of vitamin A to take care of your skin and eyes. Himalaya salt helps you add more alkaline minerals like Magnesium to help you take care of your immune system.

Servings: 2
Ingredients:
Liquid:
- 1 cup cashew milk, unsweetened, unsalted
- 2 tablespoons flax seed oil

Dry:
- 1 cup fresh parsley leaves
- 2 tablespoon fresh cilantro leaves

Other:
- Black pepper (optional)
- Himalaya salt to taste
- 2 lime slices to garnish

Instructions:
1. Place all the ingredients in a blender.
2. Process until smooth.
3. Garnish with lime slices, serve and enjoy!

Vitamin C Power House Smoothie

This recipe provides a ton of Vitamin C and is very easy to make.

You can make it on the go, using a simple hand blender or a hand processor.

Servings: 2
Ingredients:
- 1 cup thick coconut milk (full fat)
- 1 tablespoon coconut oil
- 1 lemon, peeled and sliced
- 1 tablespoon chia seed powder
- 1 teaspoon cinnamon powder
- Optional – stevia to sweeten

Instructions:
1. Place all the ingredients in a blender.
2. Process until smooth.
3. Serve and enjoy!
4. If needed sweeten with stevia.

Easy Relaxation Smoothie

Chamomile is a great choice to help you relax on a deeper level! Allowing your body to relax when needed, is also a fantastic, holistic tool to help you boost your immune system.

Servings: 2
Ingredients:
- 1 cup chamomile tea (cooled down, use 1 teabag per cup)
- 1 small avocado, peeled and pitted
- 1 small lime, peeled and sliced
- Half cup almond milk
- 1 teaspoon cinnamon powder
- Stevia to sweeten if needed

Instructions:
1. Place all the ingredients in a blender.
2. Process until smooth.
3. Relax and enjoy!

Spicy Mediterranean Smoothie

This smoothie is rich in good fats and protein and can be turned into a delicious, satisfying raw (or lightly cooked) soup.

Servings: 2
Ingredients:
- 2 green bell peppers, chopped, seeds removed
- Half avocado, peeled and pitted
- 1 small garlic clove, peeled
- Pinch of black pepper and chili
- 1 cup almond milk, unsweetened
- A handful of almonds, soaked in water for at least a few hours
- 1 tablespoon extra-virgin olive oil
- Himalaya salt to taste

Instructions:
1. Place all the ingredients in a blender.
2. Process until smooth, serve, and enjoy!

Mood Boosting Smoothie

Having a bad day? Do you need to boost your mood? Try this smoothie. It offers a healthy mix of vitamin C, energy stimulating greens, and mood-boosting cocoa.

Servings: 1-2
Ingredients:
Liquid:
- 1 cup coconut milk
- Half cup water, filtered
- 1 teaspoon coconut oil

Dry:
- 1-inch ginger, peeled
- 1-inch turmeric, peeled
- Half cup arugula leaves
- 1 orange, peeled

Other:
- Stevia to sweeten (optional)
- Half teaspoon cinnamon
- 1 tablespoon cocoa powder
- 1 tablespoon chia seeds
- A few drops of liquid chlorophyll

Instructions:

1. Blend and enjoy.
2. Add some stevia to sweeten if needed.
3. This drink is great first thing in the morning. But you can also sip on it during the day to enjoy more energy or whenever you are having a bad day!

Protein Hormone Balancer

This delicious smoothie uses maca powder, which is a hormone re-balancer for women.

Servings: 1-2
Ingredients:
Liquid:
- 1 cup coconut or almond milk (unsweetened)
- 1 tablespoon coconut oil
- Half cup coconut water

Dry:
- Half cup kale leaves
- 1 banana, peeled
- Half green apple

Other:
- A bit of stevia to sweeten
- Half teaspoon fresh maca powder
- 1 tablespoon hemp seed protein powder (personally, I like chocolate-flavored protein powder)

+ a few lime slices and ice cubes to serve if needed

Instructions:
1. Place all the ingredients in a blender.
2. Process until smooth.

3. Serve and enjoy!
4. This smoothie also tastes delicious when chilled or half-frozen.

Simple Detox Spicy Smoothie

If you are looking for a quick detox recipe-this smoothie recipe will help you sweat out all the toxins and supercharge your nutrition!

Servings: 2-3
Ingredients:
Liquid:
- 1 cup organic tomato juice
- Half cup unsweetened almond milk

Dry:
- 1 garlic clove, peeled
- Half cup arugula leaves, washed
- 1 teaspoon hemp protein powder
- 2 big cucumbers, peeled and roughly sliced
- 6 radishes, sliced
- 2 tablespoons chive, chopped

Other:
- Pinch of Himalayan salt
- Pinch of black pepper
- Pinch of chili powder

Instructions:

1. Place all the ingredients through a blender.
2. Blend, serve, and enjoy!
3. You can also serve this smoothie as a quick, raw detox soup.

Ultimate Health Smoothie

This smoothie tastes delicious, and I highly recommend it for days where your goal is detoxification to have more energy.

Servings: 2-3
Ingredients:
Liquid:

- 1 cup coconut or almond milk
- Half cup water, filtered
- 1 tablespoon coconut oil

Dry:

- 4 tablespoons almonds, chopped or powdered
- A handful of cilantro leaves
- 1 tablespoon chia seeds
- 2 big cucumbers, peeled and roughly sliced
- 1 big avocado, peeled and pitted
- Half lemon, peeled and sliced

Other:

- 2 tablespoons chive, chopped
- 1 teaspoon spirulina powder
- Pinch of Himalaya salt to taste
- Pinch of black pepper to taste

Instructions:

1.Place all the ingredients in a blender.

2.Blend well and pour into a smoothie glass or a small soup bowl.

3.Serve and enjoy!

Simple Cleanse Smoothie

This simple Vitamin C rich smoothie is quick to make and a fantastic natural detox tool.

Servings: 1-2
Ingredients:
Liquid:
- 1 cup full-fat coconut milk (no added sugar)
- Half cup of water, filtered

Dry:
- Half cup radish washed
- 1 small avocado, peeled and pitted
- A handful of fresh arugula leaves

Other:
- Pinch of Himalaya salt to taste
- 1 teaspoon chlorella
- 1 teaspoon spirulina
- 1 teaspoon chia seeds

Instructions:
1.Blend all the ingredients.
2.Serve in a smoothie glass or in a soup bowl- this smoothie can also be turned into a delicious soup.

Super Antioxidant Green Smoothie

Cilantro is a miraculous alkaline herb with potent antioxidant properties. It tastes great in smoothies! Especially when backed up with creamy nut milk and some spices and superfoods to help you thrive!

Servings: 2-3
Ingredients:
Liquid:

- 2 cups gluten-free oat milk (or any other plant-based milk)
- 1 tablespoon coconut oil

Dry:

- A handful of fresh cilantro leaves
- 2 small carrots, peeled

Other:

- 1 teaspoon moringa
- Half teaspoon cinnamon powder
- Pinch of Himalaya salt to taste
- 1 teaspoon chlorella
- Half teaspoon Ashwagandha

Instructions:
1.Combine all the ingredients in a blender.
2.Process until smooth. Enjoy!

Fill Me Up Smoothie

This smoothie is rich in good fats and very low in carbs. At the same time, it incorporates a myriad of different nutrient-packed superfoods. The perfect recipe to fill you up and help you stay healthy.

Servings: 2
Ingredients:
Liquid:

- 1 cup of coconut milk
- Half cup cashew milk
- 2 teaspoons olive oil

Dry:

- 1 big avocado, peeled, pitted and sliced
- Half lemon, peeled and sliced
- A handful of cashews
- A handful of almonds

Other:

- 1 teaspoon spirulina
- 1 teaspoon chlorella
- Himalayan salt to taste

Instructions:
1.Place all the ingredients in a blender.
2.Process until smooth. Serve and enjoy!

Recipes

Sweet Veggie Smoothie

This smoothie is naturally sweet even though it doesn't use any fruit. It's because red bell peppers are naturally delicious veggies. Then, coconut water adds in a more natural sweet taste, while stevia and cinnamon take it to the next level.

Servings: 1-2
Ingredients:
Liquid:
- 2 cups of coconut water
- 1 tablespoon coconut oil

Dry:
- 1 big red bell pepper
- 2 medium-size carrots, peeled
- Half avocado, peeled and sliced

Other:
- Half teaspoon moringa powder
- Half teaspoon spirulina powder
- Half teaspoon cinnamon powder
- Stevia to sweeten, if needed

Instructions:
1. Blend all the ingredients in a blender. Enjoy!

Green Energy Bowl

This green smoothie bowl is rich in fiber, good protein, healthy fats, and energizing greens. A perfect way to take care of your immune system in a deeply holistic way.

Servings: 1-2
Ingredients:
Liquid:

- 1 cup coconut milk
- 1 teaspoon coconut oil or avocado oil

Dry:

- A handful of dates, pitted
- Half cup spinach leaves, washed
- 1 tablespoon sunflower seeds
- 1 tablespoon raisins
- 1 tablespoon crushed almonds

Other:

- Half teaspoon cinnamon powder
- Optional: 1 teaspoon Organifi powder (you can learn more at www.YourWellnessBooks.com/resources)

Instructions:
1. Blend all the ingredients (except sunflower seeds, raisins, and almonds) in a blender.
2. Pour your smoothie into a smoothie bowl.
3. Place the sunflower seeds, raisins, and crushed almonds in a smoothie bowl.
4. Serve and enjoy!

Anti-Flu Green Abundance Smoothie

This recipe uses healing alkaline veggies like cauliflower, and, at the same time, adds in some garlic to help you strengthen your immune system. You can also use it as a nutritious meal replacement.

Servings: 1-2
Ingredients:
Liquid:
- 2 cups almond milk
- 1 tablespoon olive oil

Dry:
- half cup cauliflower, slightly cooked or steamed, cut into smaller pieces
- 2 garlic cloves, peeled
- 1 cup arugula leaves
- One small chili flake (optional)

Other:
- Himalaya salt
- Half teaspoon curry powder
- Half teaspoon turmeric powder with a pinch of black pepper
- 1 teaspoon chlorella

Instructions:

1. Place all the ingredients in a blender.
2. Blend until smooth, serve and enjoy!

Conclusion

Your body is smart. It wants to stay healthy and keep you happy. You just need to nourish it from the inside out! So, give it exactly what it needs and make it thrive.

Here's to a happier, healthier life!

We are in this together,
Thank you for reading to the end,

Elena

We Need Your Help

One more thing, before you go, could you please do us a quick favor?

It would be great if you could leave us a short review online.

Don't worry, it doesn't have to be long. One sentence is enough.

Let others know your favorite recipes and who you think this book can help.

Thank You for your support!

(if you have any questions about this book, you can also email us at: info@yourwellnessbooks.com)

Join Our VIP Readers' Newsletter to Boost Your Wellbeing

Would you like to be notified about our new health and wellness books? How about receiving them at deeply discounted prices? What about awesome giveaways, latest health tips, and motivation? If that is something you are interested in, please visit the link below to join our newsletter:

www.yourwellnessbooks.com/email-newsletter

As a bonus, you will receive a free complimentary eBook *Alkaline Paleo Superfoods*

Sign up link:

www.yourwellnessbooks.com/email-newsletter

More Books & Resources in the Healthy Lifestyle Series

Available at:

www.yourwellnessbooks.com